SOUPS
～ from ～
the Market

Brad McCrorie

DOUBLEDAY CANADA LIMITED

CANADIAN CATALOGUING IN PUBLICATION DATA
McCrorie, Brad
Soups from the market

Includes index.
ISBN 0-385-25393-1

1. Soups. I. Title.

TX757.M37 1992   641.8'13   C92-094626-7

Designed by Tania Craan
Cover photograph courtesy
Fred Bird/Canadian Living
Printed and bound in the USA

Published in Canada by
Doubleday Canada Limited
105 Bond Street
Toronto, Ontario
M5B 1Y3

CONTENTS

Introduction

We can never, it seems, get too much of a good thing.

What music lover wouldn't delight in hearing just one more Mozart concerto or Beethoven sonata? Where is the film-goer who can resist yet another sequel to *Rocky* or *Star Trek*? And where are they who fail to be excited by the promise of a new video by Madonna or Michael Jackson or a concert tour by a legend such as Sinatra or Streisand?

It's in this spirit that we present the sequel to *Soups For All Seasons*, Chef Brad's best-selling cookbook of 1987.

Soups are wonderfully delicious and nutritious, spring, summer, autumn and winter. Whether as the first course in a feast or as the main course of a light lunch, they satisfy in ways few other foods can match, delighting the palate while seeming to touch our very soul. Few are we who, while enjoying a hot and hearty bowl of soup on a cold winter's day, don't find our minds wandering back to days of childhood and the delights of homemade soup on the stove to warm us up after hours on the ice rink or ski slopes.

In fact, the only quarrel one might have would be with the word *soup*, itself. It seems such a plain name for so complex a creation. To call Chef Brad's Crab with Cream and Garlic (p. 36) a mere soup is like referring to Rodgers and Hammerstein's Soliloquy from Carousel as a mere *song*. Both are more – much more – than any four-letter word can suggest.

If you've had the delight of tasting Chef Brad's soups you know what we mean. And if you're among the many who have read and used the original Doubleday Canada publication, *Soups For All Seasons*, you already know the basic secrets that make Chef Brad's soups so extraordinary.

The secrets are three. First, start with your own stock. Second, always use fresh ingredients. And third, be imaginative.

On the pages immediately following, Chef Brad takes the mystery out of preparing your own stocks, sauces and thickeners. It's not as difficult as you may think, but it's as important as market-fresh ingredients. Make shopping for fresh ingredients an adventure, as Chef Brad does daily. Don't decide in advance what soup you're going to make that day. Let the availability of the best and freshest vegetables and fish and meats dictate that decision to you on a seasonal basis. What better reason for preparing Chef Brad's B.C. Salmon with Saffron and Lemon Juice (p.22) than the arrival of fresh B.C. salmon at your local fish market?

As for imagination, that's what *Soups from the Market* is all about. Here you'll find fifty of the most imaginative recipes that have sprung from Chef Brad's creative mind.

In the five years since *Soups For All Seasons* was published, chef Brad McCrorie's reputation on the Canadian cooking scene has grown from that of a talented and promising newcomer to that of a respected and highly-acclaimed master of the culinary arts.

A soup of his creation won the Best of Show Coca-Cola Classic Award at the Royal Winter Fair, leading to an invitation for him to be a member of Canada's Olympic Cooking Team.

A second book of his recipes was published by Doubleday Canada, called *Fresh From The Market: Adventures in Creative Cooking*. It was immediately acclaimed by the press and quickly became another best-seller.

He has become a popular guest on television and radio, appearing on the CTV programs "Lifetime," "Eye on Toronto" and "Toronto Today," on the Global network's "News At Noon," on CITY-TV's "Breakfast Television" and "The Dini Petty Show," on CKVR-TV in Barrie, and on radio stations ranging from CBC to CKO. In fact, his appearance on "The Jeremy Brown Show" resulted in that program's largest-ever phone-in response, so taken were listeners by his outspoken views on food preparation.

He is also in demand as a teacher, most recently conducting an eight-week gourmet cooking school at Toronto's Columbus Centre.

You can never get too much of a good thing.

Some Terms and Techniques

Unsalted Butter
Since the addition of salt to any food or soup is ultimately a matter of taste or diet, the recipes in this book were tested using unsalted butter. Salted butter, for those who prefer it, can be substituted.

Clarified Butter
This is butter from which the butter fat and milk solids have been removed. It is made by melting butter over a medium-high heat, then skimming off or straining the solids from the resulting liquid. Used for flavor and color when browning or frying, clarified butter gives the cook the ability to cook longer, at higher temperatures, without burning.

Commercial Bases
Time is an important ingredient in any cook's plans for dinner. Since few people have enough of it to devote to the proper reduction of the stocks used in the soup recipes in this book, there is no harm in adding one or two tablespoons of commercial base for added flavor when and where time and taste dictate.

Adding Cheese or Eggs to Soup
Cheese is only added to cream soups or soups that contain plenty of ingredients for the cheese to cling to. Cheese is always grated before it is added to the boiling broth. Eggs must be added slowly with a whisk while the soup or stock

is boiling. Soups may also be thickened without flour by a liaison of equal parts egg yolk and whipping cream (35 percent). This mixture should be added once the soup has been brought to a boil and whisked in slowly (not whipped) with the heat reduced to simmer.

Dried Mushrooms

Some of the recipes featured in this book call for dried mushrooms. This is simply because dried mushrooms are available all year round. Dried mushrooms should always be soaked for at least an hour at room temperature in water that has been brought to a rapid boil, then removed from the heat. Since the stems of dried mushrooms are apt to be tough, always trim the ends of the stems, or remove the stems altogether.

Freezing Soups

Since cream added to the stock in the preparation of creamed soups is apt to separate when frozen, it is best not to freeze creamed soups. However, you can always freeze the stock from which you plan to make a creamed soup. When the soup is thawed, add the cream to the stock when it comes to a boil. Since crisp vegetables will not be crisp when frozen and later reheated, and since eggs will discolor, clear soups should only be frozen after straining out these ingredients. Fresh vegetables or eggs can then be added, according to the recipe, once the stock has been thawed and brought to the proper temperature.

Reduction

Stocks, soups and even wines are reduced by simmering to increase, strengthen or concentrate their flavor. Reductions called for in each recipe (one-half reduction/one-quarter reduction) are achieved by simmering the liquid over a medium-high heat to the desired strength.

Roux

Light or dark, roux are easy to make and are often used to thicken soup. Both call for equal parts of butter and flour blended gently over a slow heat until the flour is cooked enough to rid it of its starchy taste. For the rich, nutty flavor of dark roux – used in thick, dark, and gamey soups – cook the roux over a medium-high heat until it turns a rich brown color.

Sauté, Sweat

To sauté is to cook food rapidly in hot butter or fat, turning and tossing it until it is golden brown, thereby sealing in the juices. To sweat is to bleed the juices from vegetables by stirring them gently in hot butter.

Serving Sizes

All the soups in this book will yield 8- to 10-ounce servings – perfect for lunch, pre-dinner, or a meal at any time.

Deglaze

Deglazing is a technique for removing all the drippings from a roasting pan. After the food has been removed from the roasting pan, pour wine or stock onto the pan while it is still hot. Scrape the mixture of wine or stock and remaining ingredients from the bottom of the pan and preserve this wonderful mixture. It can be added to a stock, or used as the essence of a sauce.

Tomato Concassée

Only the meat of the tomato is used in concassée. To remove the seeds and skin, cut out the core of the tomato and make two shallow cuts just piercing the skin. Drop tomatoes into boiling water, and cook for one minute. Remove from the water and peel the skin away with a paring knife. The tomatoes will be quite hot, so wear rubber gloves. Cut the tomatoes in half and squeeze seeds out very gently. Dice the tomato meat, and the concassée is ready.

Sauces, Stocks and Thickeners

Beurre Manié

Beurre manié is made with equal parts of whole butter and hard white flour, kneaded together until all the lumps disappear and it forms a smooth paste. It is a good idea for the serious cook to keep a pound of this excellent thickener in the refrigerator. When beurre manié is stored this way, it should be brought to room temperature before using. Since the flour is raw and apt to lump when added to hot liquids, one cup of the soup or stock should be added to the beurre manié a little at a time, stirring constantly until the mixture is consistent. It is then ready to be added to the cooking pot. Remember that raw flour needs to be cooked thoroughly to remove the starchy taste.

Sauce Velouté

Bring either veal, chicken or fish stock to a boil. Slowly whisk in about ½ cup (125 mL) beurre manié to the boiling stock, until it reaches the thickness you desire. Remove from heat.

Stock and Demi-Glace

Following are three basic recipes used throughout the book: chicken stock, beef stock and beef demi-glace. Recipes that use special vegetable, fish, poultry or game stocks have the stock recipe included with the soup recipe.

Fonds Blanc, Veal or Chicken Stock

Quantities for this stock are not exact. A pot that easily holds 16 cups (4 L) of water should yield about 12 cups (3 L) of stock. For veal stock, use shank bones. For chicken stock, use combinations of necks, backs, wings, legs and feet. If you desire a white stock, do not brown the bones first.

Wash, peel and chop vegetables (onions, carrots, celery, garlic and leeks). Make a small bag of cheese cloth, and fill it with thyme, basil, bay leaves, oregano and whole black peppercorns. This is called a bouquet garni. Place all the ingredients in a large pot and cover with cold water. Place on top of the stove at high heat and bring to a boil. Reduce the heat and simmer for 2 hours or longer if you wish.

Strain stock and let it cool. Stock is now ready to be stored in portions in the refrigerator or the freezer for future use.

Demi-Glace or Basic Brown Sauce
Bring 8 cups (2 L) of a hearty beef stock to a boil. When stock reaches the boil, put a heavy frying pan on high heat. Heat 4 oz (116 g) of clarified butter in the frying pan, then add 4 oz (116 g) of hard white flour. Cook the roux until golden brown, and stir it constantly to avoid burning.

When brown, slowly ladle one cup of the stock into the hot roux, stirring constantly with a whisk to avoid lumps. When the stock and roux mixture has blended into a smooth paste, then it can be added to the stock. When the stock combination has returned to the boil, your demi-glace is complete.

Fish Stock

2 lbs	grouper head	1 kg
2–3 lbs	white fish or their bones	1–1.5 kg
3	carrots, peeled and coarsely chopped	3
1	large spanish onion, peeled and coarsely chopped	1
6	large garlic cloves, peeled	6
10	white peppercorns	10
8	bay leaves	8
	salt to taste	

Place all the ingredients into a large pot on top of the stove on high heat. Add cold water to cover ingredients by 1 inch. Bring to a rolling boil. Remove from the stove and let stand for 20 minutes. Strain through a china cap, a fine meshed, cone-shaped strainer or use a colander.

Fond De Gibier or Game Stock
(For game or fowl)

Place about 2 lbs (1 kg) of game bones – preferably with marrow – on a flat baking tray and put into a preheated 450°F (230°C) oven for 1 hour to brown. Add a *mirepoix*, made up of carrots, onion, celery and garlic which have been coarsely chopped, and bake for an additional 30 minutes. Remove, and reserve all the ingredients. Deglaze tray with red wine, and put this mixture into a pot that easily holds 16 cups (4 L). To the pot, add the bones and vegetables, along with 6 bay leaves, 20 juniper berries, 1 tsp (5 mL) thyme and 2 tsp (10 mL) tarragon. Fill the pot to several inches below rim with cold water and bring to the boil on high heat. When boiling begins, turn heat down and let simmer until reduced by one-third.

Basic Beef Stock

3 lbs	beef bones	1.5 kg
2	onions with skin, quartered	2
2	carrots, cut in	2
	2-inch (5-cm) pieces	
3	garlic cloves	3
2	celery stalks, cut in	2
	2-inch (5 cm) pieces	
2 Tbsp	tomato paste	30 mL
12 cups	cold water	3 L

Preheat oven to 450°F (250°C).

Place bones in a shallow roasting pan. Roast in preheated oven until they begin to brown, about 30 minutes. Add onions, carrots, garlic, celery and tomato paste and continue to roast about 30 minutes more or until bones and vegetables are dark brown.

Combine browned bones and vegetables with water in a large stock pot. Bring to a boil over medium-high heat. Reduce heat to medium-low and simmer for 1 to 2 hours, skimming off the foam as it appears, and adding more water as necessary to keep the level constant. Strain out the bones and vegetables.

Yields 12 cups (3 L)

Note: For the richest stock, oxtails should be used.

Basic Chicken Stock

4.4 lbs	chicken bones	2 kg
2	onions with skin, quartered	2
3	carrots, cut in 2-inch (5-cm) pieces	3
3	garlic cloves with their skin	3
2	celery stalks, cut in 2-inch (5-cm) chunks	2
2	bay leaves	2
¼ tsp	dried basil	1 mL
¼ tsp	dried oregano	1 mL
¼ tsp	dried thyme	1 mL
1½ tsp	white peppercorns	7 mL
5	sprigs of parsley with their stems	5
16 cups	cold water	4 L

Put chicken bones, onions, carrots, garlic, celery, bay leaves, basil, oregano, thyme, peppercorns and parsley into a large, heavy stock pot and cover with water. Bring to a boil over high heat, then immediately reduce heat to medium-low and simmer for 1 or 2 hours (or longer), skimming off the foam as it appears and adding water as necessary to keep the level constant. Strain out bones and vegetables and discard them.

Return stock to pot, raise heat to medium, and cook until stock has reduced by about a quarter, about 30 minutes.

Yields 12 cups (3 L)

VEGETABLE
SOUPS

French Onion with Whole Spring Onions

An innovative variation on a classical theme that will delight the taste buds of French onion soup lovers from Montmartre to Montreal.

1 lb	whole baby onions, peeled	500 g
1 Tbsp	tomato paste	15 mL
⅓ cup	dry white wine	75 mL
6	juniper berries	6
4	bay leaves	4
1 tsp	fresh thyme	5 mL
2	garlic cloves, minced	2
8 cups	chicken stock	2 L
1	french stick, cut into	1
	½-inch thick medallions	
1¼ cups	grated Swiss cheese	300 mL
½ cup	grated Parmesan cheese	125 mL
¼ cup	dry sherry	50 mL

Combine onions, tomato paste, wine, juniper berries, bay leaves, thyme, garlic and stock in a medium-sized stock pot and bring to a boil. Reduce the heat and simmer for 45 minutes or until onions are tender.

Ladle soup into 8–9 oz (250–280 g) heat-resistant crocks. Top with a bread round. Combine cheeses and top bread round with a heaping mound of cheese. Place in preheated 450°F (230°C) oven and bake for 8–10 minutes or until browned and bubbly. Splash the top with sherry before serving.

MAKES 8–10 SERVINGS

Lentils with Smoked Pork and Strawberries

Again Chef Brad's innovative approach will delight. Combining lentils and bacon is instinctive, but adding strawberries is positively inspired.

¼ cup	clarified butter	50 mL
1 cup	diced double smoked bacon	250 mL
1 cup	sliced chanterelle mushrooms	250 mL
½ cup	sliced leek	125 mL
½ cup	diced green pepper	125 mL
½ cup	diced fennel	125 mL
1	garlic clove, minced	1
½ cup	sliced celery	125 mL
½ cup	diced onion	125 mL
¼ cup	brandy	50 mL
1 Tbsp	chopped fresh rosemary	15 mL
2 cups	sliced strawberries	500 mL
½ cup	dried lentils	125 mL
8 cups	chicken stock	2 L
	salt and pepper to taste	

Heat butter in a large soup pot. Add bacon, chanterelles, leek, green pepper, fennel, garlic, celery and onion and sauté 5 minutes. Add brandy, then stir in rosemary, strawberries, lentils and stock. Bring to a boil, then reduce the heat to simmer and cook 45 minutes. Season with salt and pepper.

MAKES 6–8 SERVINGS

Belgian Endive with Lemon, Lime and Cream

The sophistication of continental Europe combines with the tanginess of Florida in the creation of this creamy delight.

3 Tbsp	clarified butter	45 mL
½ cup	chopped onion	125 mL
¼ cup	diced red pepper	50 mL
1 Tbsp	chopped fresh dill	15 mL
4 cups	chicken stock	1 L
	juice of 1 lemon	
	juice of 2 limes	
3 cups	sliced Belgian endive	750 mL
¼ cup	beurre manié	50 mL
⅓ cup	heavy cream (35%)	75 mL
	salt, pepper and nutmeg to taste	

In a medium soup pot heat butter over medium heat. Add onion, pepper and dill and sauté 3–4 minutes. Add stock, lemon and lime juices and Belgian endive. Bring to a boil and cook for 2–3 minutes.

Meanwhile in a small bowl whisk the beurre manié until smooth. Slowly whisk in a cupful of the soup then whisk the mixture back into soup 1 spoonful at a time, whisking constantly. Simmer 3–4 minutes or until thickened slightly. Stir in cream and season with salt, pepper and nutmeg.

MAKES 4–6 SERVINGS

Corn with Fresh Basil and Lemon

A late summer treat when the corn in Canada, like that in Oklahoma, grows "as high as an elephant's eye." And as mouth-wateringly good.

3 Tbsp	clarified butter	45 mL
4 cups	corn niblets (cut off about 8 ears of corn)	1 L
½ cup	diced green pepper	125 mL
½ cup	diced red pepper	125 mL
½ cup	diced Spanish onion	125 mL
½ cup	diced leek	125 mL
2 Tbsp	chopped fresh basil	30 mL
6 cups	chicken stock	1.5 L
	juice of 2 large lemons	
1 tsp	white sugar	5 mL
	salt and white pepper to taste	

Heat butter in a medium-sized soup pot over medium-high heat. Add the corn and sauté for 4–5 minutes, stirring occasionally. Add peppers, onion, leek and basil and continue to sauté for 2–3 minutes. Stir in stock and bring to the boil. Add lemon juice and sugar and season with salt and pepper. Reduce heat and simmer for 5 minutes. Ladle into bowls and serve.

MAKES 6 SERVINGS

Greek Eggplant Soup

*Positively Epicurean. Your dinner guests are
likely to think you discovered this recipe in some
quaint little bistro overlooking the Aegean.
Why tell them differently?*

3 Tbsp	olive oil	45 mL
4 cups	coarsely diced eggplant	1 L
½ cup	sliced leeks	125 mL
3	garlic cloves, minced	3
1 cup	sliced stuffed pimento olives	250 mL
1 Tbsp	chopped fresh oregano	15 mL
8 cups	chicken stock	2 L
½ lb	Feta cheese, crumbled	250 g
	juice of 1 lemon (or to taste)	
	salt and white pepper to taste	

Heat olive oil in a medium soup pot over medium heat.
Add eggplant, leek, garlic, olives and oregano and sweat for
8–10 minutes, stirring frequently. Add stock and bring to
a boil. Then reduce the heat and simmer 3–4 minutes.
Whisk in cheese and season with lemon juice, salt and
pepper.

MAKES 8 SERVINGS

Spanish Onion and Bean Soup

*Trumpets herald the arrival of the matador in his
suit of lights to a dusty bullring in southern
Spain—and the crowd goes wild. So will your
family when they taste this sunny treat.*

1 cup	dried white beans	250 mL
2	garlic cloves, minced	2
¼ cup	lard	50 mL
½ cup	chopped onion	125 mL
1	small cabbage, shredded	1
11 cups	beef stock	2.75 L
	salt and pepper to taste	

In a large non-metallic bowl, cover beans and garlic with cold water. Soak overnight. In a medium-sized soup pot heat the lard over medium-high heat. Add the onion and sauté for 3–4 minutes, stirring occasionally. Add cabbage, drained beans with garlic and stock. Bring to a boil, then reduce heat and simmer about 3 hours or until beans are tender. Season with salt and pepper.

MAKES 6–8 SERVINGS

Whole Mushrooms in Broth

*The simplicity and earthiness of a poem by
Henry David Thoreau is captured by
Chef Brad in a broth that bubbles to the
beat of a different drummer.*

¼ cup	clarified butter	50 mL
40	fresh mushrooms, medium sized	40
1 cup	diced fresh red pepper	250 mL
1 cup	diced leek	250 mL
1	garlic clove, minced	1
2 Tbsp	long grain rice	30 mL
¼ cup	chopped fresh basil	50 mL
¼ cup	dry sherry	50 mL
¼ cup	dry white wine	50 mL
1 Tbsp	Dijon mustard	15 mL
6 cups	chicken stock	1.5 L
	salt and white pepper to taste	

In a medium-sized soup pot heat butter over medium heat. Add mushrooms, red pepper, leek, garlic and rice and sauté 4–5 minutes, stirring occasionally. Add basil, sherry, wine, mustard and stock. Bring to a boil, then turn down heat to simmer for 20 minutes. Season with salt and pepper.

MAKES 4–6 SERVINGS

Oyster Mushrooms with Tomato

*The "My Fair Lady" of soups—the humble,
lowborn mushroom elevated to the heights of
dinner party elegance. Luvverly!*

¼ cup	olive oil	50 mL
25	large oyster mushrooms, sliced	25
3	garlic cloves, minced	3
½ cup	diced onion	125 mL
½ cup	diced green pepper	125 mL
½ cup	diced fennel	125 mL
2 cups	tomato concassée	500 mL
4 cups	chicken stock	1 L
1 tsp	sugar	5 ml
	salt and white pepper to taste	

Heat oil in a small soup pot over medium-high heat. Add mushrooms, garlic, onion, green pepper and fennel and sweat for 3–4 minutes, stirring occasionally. Add tomato concassée and stock. Bring to a boil, reduce heat and simmer 10 minutes. Stir in sugar and season with salt and pepper.

MAKES 4 SERVINGS

Cream of Brussels Sprouts and Gorgonzola

You say you have youngsters who don't like Brussels sprouts? Simply don't tell them what this soup is—until after they've eaten it and asked for a second helping!

⅓ cup	clarified butter	75 mL
½ lb	Brussels sprouts, trimmed	250 g
1 cup	chopped onion	250 mL
4 cups	chicken stock	1 L
¼ cup	vermicelli	50 mL
⅓ cup	heavy cream (35%)	75 mL
¼ cup	crumbled Gorgonzola	50 mL
	pepper to taste	

In a small saucepan heat 3 Tbsp (40 mL) of the butter. Add Brussels sprouts and cook for 10–15 minutes over medium heat. Meanwhile, heat remaining butter in a medium-sized soup pot, then add onion and sauté for 4–5 minutes. Add the stock to the onion and simmer for 10 minutes. Add Brussels sprouts and vermicelli and simmer until noodles are fully cooked. Stir in cream, Gorgonzola and season with pepper.

MAKES 4–6 SERVINGS

Olde Fashioned
Corn Chowder

*A classic. The Indians were preparing and
enjoying corn chowders long before the arrival
of Europeans in Canada. But we doubt theirs
was quite as good as this.*

3 Tbsp	clarified butter	45 mL
3 cups	corn niblets (cut off about 6 ears of corn)	750 mL
½ cup	sliced celery	125 mL
½ cup	diced red pepper	125 mL
½ cup	diced green pepper	125 mL
½ cup	chopped onion	125 mL
1	garlic clove, minced	1
4 cups	chicken stock	1 L
¼ cup	beurre manié	50 mL
½ cup	heavy cream (35%)	125 mL
1 Tbsp	brown sugar	15 mL
3 dashes	Worcestershire sauce	3 dashes
pinch	dry mustard	pinch
pinch	nutmeg	pinch
	salt and pepper to taste	

Heat butter in a medium-sized soup pot over medium heat.
Add corn, celery, peppers, onion and garlic and sauté for

4–5 minutes. Add stock and bring to a boil then reduce the heat and simmer for 8–10 minutes.

Meanwhile in a small bowl whisk the beurre manié until smooth. Slowly whisk in a cupful of soup until a smooth mixture is formed. Slowly whisk back into soup 1 spoonful at a time, whisking constantly. Stir in cream and sugar and season with Worcestershire, mustard, nutmeg, salt and pepper.

MAKES 6 SERVINGS

Braised Garlic Bordelaise

*Chef Brad's love of garlic is requited
with this recipe in which garlic is not a mere
supporting player but the star of the show,
just for a change of pace.*

1	beef shank	1
2 Tbsp	clarified butter	30 mL
½ cup	chopped onion	125 mL
½ cup	diced green pepper	125 mL
½ cup	diced leek	125 mL
14	garlic cloves, peeled	14
¼ cup	port wine	50 mL
1 Tbsp	green peppercorns in brine	15 mL
7 cups	beef stock	1.75 L
2 Tbsp	chopped fresh thyme	30 mL

Have your butcher cut a beef shank into 1-inch thick pieces.
Place the bones in a medium-sized roasting pan and roast in
a preheated 400°F (200°C) oven for 20–30 minutes; cool. In
a medium soup pot, heat butter; sauté onion, green pepper
and leek for 4–5 minutes, stirring frequently. Add garlic,
port, green peppercorns, stock and thyme. Bring to a boil,
then reduce heat and simmer for 5 minutes.

Meanwhile separate the marrow from the bones and add
the marrow to the broth. Allow 2–3 cloves of garlic per person.

MAKES 4–6 SERVINGS

SEAFOOD
SOUPS

Fresh Tuna with Whole Capers and Sherry

*They that "go down to the sea in ships" and
"do business in great waters" are lauded not only
in the psalms of David but also by those who
feast on this soup by Chef Brad.*

¼ cup	clarified butter	50 mL
¾ lb	fresh tuna, cut in ½-inch chunks	375 g
½ cup	chopped onion	125 mL
1	garlic clove, minced	1
1 tsp	chopped fresh tarragon	5 mL
35	capers	35
¼ cup	dry sherry	50 mL
4 cups	chicken stock	1 L
3 Tbsp	beurre manié	45 mL
¼ cup	heavy cream (35%)	50 mL
1 tsp	Dijon mustard	5 mL
	salt, pepper and nutmeg to taste	

Melt the butter in a medium soup pot over medium heat. Add the tuna and sauté for 2–3 minutes. Add onion, garlic, tarragon and capers and sauté 2–3 minutes more. Stir in the sherry and stock, and bring to a boil.

Meanwhile whisk beurre manié until smooth. Slowly whisk a cupful of soup stock into the beurre manié until a smooth paste is formed. Whisk the mixture back into soup pot 1 spoonful at a time. Stir in the cream and mustard and season with salt, pepper and nutmeg.

MAKES 4 SERVINGS

Crab à la King

The crab may be king but the pimento olive is his consort in this most regal of soups. Neptune himself would approve.

¼ cup	clarified butter	50 mL
1	garlic clove, minced	1
½ cup	diced onion	125 mL
30	stuffed green olives	30
½ cup	diced green pepper	125 mL
2 lbs	king crab legs — cut into 2-inch pieces	1 kg
½ cup	chopped fresh basil	125 mL
¼ cup	dry white wine	50 mL
¼ cup	dry red wine	50 mL
6 cups	chicken stock	1.5 L
¼ cup	beurre manié	50 mL
⅓ cup	heavy cream (35%)	75 mL
½ cup	grated Romano cheese	125 mL

Heat butter in a large soup pot. Add garlic, onion, olives and green pepper and sauté for 2 minutes. Add the crab and basil and sauté for 2–3 minutes, stirring occasionally. Add wines and stock and bring to a boil.

Meanwhile whisk beurre manié in a medium bowl until smooth. Slowly whisk in a cupful of soup. Add the mixture 1 spoonful at a time back into soup. Whisk in saffron, cream and cheese. Simmer for 2–3 minutes and serve.

MAKES 8 SERVINGS

Scallops with Two Mushrooms in Red Wine

The choicest fruits of the sea swimming in the fermented juices of the finest fruits off the vine. Very French. Très, très bon.

1 pkg	(⅙ oz/5 gr) dried yellow bolet mushrooms	1 pkg
1 pkg	(⅙ oz/5 gr) dried cep mushrooms	1 pkg
⅓ cup	red wine	75 mL
2 Tbsp	cognac	30 mL
¼ cup	clarified butter	50 mL
1 lb	bay scallops	500 g
½ cup	diced onion	125 mL
½ cup	diced pimento or red pepper	125 mL
1	garlic clove, minced	1
1 tsp	chopped fresh tarragon	5 mL
3 cups	chicken stock	750 mL
2 Tbsp	beurre manié	30 mL
¼ cup	heavy cream (35%)	50 mL
	salt and pepper to taste	

Soak the mushrooms in wine and cognac for 1 hour. Heat the butter in a medium soup pot over medium-high heat. Add scallops, onion, pimento and garlic and sauté for 3–4 minutes. Add mushrooms, wine and cognac and simmer until reduced by half. Stir in tarragon and stock and bring to a boil.

Meanwhile in a small bowl whisk beurre manié until smooth. Slowly whisk in one cupful of soup. Whisk mixture back into soup. Stir in cream and season with salt and pepper.

MAKES 4 SERVINGS

B.C. Salmon with Saffron and Lemon Juice

Any British Columbia salmon suspecting it might come to such an elegant end would swim upstream all the sooner and faster, we suspect.

¼ cup	clarified butter	50 mL
¾ lb	B.C. salmon cut into ½-inch cubes	375 g
1	garlic clove, minced	1
½ cup	finely diced onion	125 mL
½ cup	finely diced leek	125 mL
½ cup	finely diced pimento or red pepper	125 mL
	juice of 1 lemon	
6–8	threads of saffron	6–8
3 cups	clear fish stock	750 mL
½ cup	roasted pine nuts white pepper to taste	125 mL

Heat butter in a small soup pot over medium-high heat. Add salmon, garlic, onion, leek and pimento and sauté for 3–4 minutes, stirring frequently. Add lemon juice, saffron and stock. Bring to a boil, reduce heat and simmer for three minutes. Ladle into bowls and garnish with pine nuts.

MAKES 3–4 SERVINGS

Cream of Smoked Salmon with Fresh Dill and Cognac

The publisher has his opinion. This writer has his own. This is his choice as his favorite for all seasons. So simple to prepare yet so very sophisticated.

2 Tbsp	clarified butter	30 mL
1	garlic clove, minced	1
¼ cup	finely diced onion	50 mL
2 tsp	finely diced pimento or red pepper	10 mL
10 oz	diced smoked salmon	300 g
1 tsp	chopped fresh dill	5 mL
2 Tbsp	cognac	30 mL
2 cups	fish velouté	500 mL
2 ½ cups	fish stock	625 mL
	freshly ground pepper	

Heat butter in a small pot. Add garlic, onion, pimento and sweat for 3–4 minutes over medium heat. Add salmon and dill and continue to cook for 2 minutes, stirring constantly. Add cognac, fish velouté and stock. Bring to a boil, then reduce heat, simmer for 2–3 minutes and serve.

MAKES 2-4 SERVINGS

Tandoori Lobster
with Red Lentils

That most elegant of expatriate Trinidadians,
Grace, maîtresse d' at the Market Street Bistro,
gives this a five-star rating. So do we.
So will you.

¼ cup	clarified butter	50 mL
¾ lb	lobster tail, chopped in ¼-inch pieces	375 g
3	garlic cloves, minced	3
1 cup	chopped leek	250 mL
1 cup	chopped onion	250 mL
1 cup	chopped green pepper	250 mL
1 cup	chopped celery	250 mL
½ cup	red lentils (fully cooked)	125 mL
2 Tbsp	tandoori barbecue marinade powder	30 mL
2 Tbsp	Trinidad hot sauce	30 mL
5 cups	chicken stock	1.25 L
	salt and pepper to taste	

Heat butter in a medium-sized soup pot over medium heat.
Add lobster, garlic, leek, onion, green pepper and celery
and sauté for 3–4 minutes. Add lentils, tandoori marinade,
hot sauce and stock. Bring to the boil, reduce heat and
simmer for 5 minutes or until lentils are heated. Season
with salt and pepper.

MAKES 4–6 SERVINGS

Scallops with Yellow Ceps and Red Wine

A treat suitable for Mardi Gras and other festive occasions. The flavor of Dixieland music in a bowl.

1 pkg	(approx. ⅓ oz/10 g) dried yellow cep mushrooms	1 pkg
½ cup	red wine	125 mL
¼ cup	clarified butter	50 mL
½ cup	finely chopped onion	125 mL
¼ cup	finely diced red pepper	50 mL
¼ cup	finely diced green pepper	50 mL
1	garlic clove, minced	1
½ lb	fresh bay scallops	250 g
1 tsp	tomato paste	5 mL
1 tsp	chopped fresh thyme	5 mL
2 cups	fish velouté	500 mL
	salt and pepper to taste	

In a small bowl cover ceps with wine and soak at least 1 hour. In a small soup pot heat butter, add onion, peppers and garlic and sauté for 3–4 minutes. Add scallops and cook for 2 minutes, stirring constantly (scallops should not finish cooking). Add ceps, wine, tomato paste, thyme and velouté and stir well. Bring mixture just to the boil, season with salt and pepper and serve. (Be sure not to over-cook scallops.)

MAKES 4 SERVINGS

Marlin with Green Olives and Cream

What better excuse could you have to head down Mexico way for a day of deep-sea fishing than your need for fresh marlin to bring this recipe to life?

¼ cup	clarified butter	50 mL
1¼ lbs	marlin, in ¼-inch cubes	625 g
½ cup	chopped green olives	125 mL
½ cup	diced onion	125 mL
1	garlic clove, minced	1
½ cup	diced red pepper	125 mL
1 tsp	chopped fresh tarragon	5 mL
¼ cup	cognac	50 mL
¼ cup	dry white wine	50 mL
6 cups	fish or chicken stock	1.5 L
2 Tbsp	beurre manié	30 mL
¼ cup	heavy cream (35%)	50 mL
	salt and white pepper to taste	

Melt butter in a medium soup pot. Add marlin and sauté for 2–3 minutes. Add olives, onion, garlic, red pepper and tarragon and sauté for 2–3 minutes. Add cognac, wine and stock and bring to a boil. Whisk beurre manié until smooth. Slowly whisk in a cupful of soup. Whisk the mixture back into soup 1 spoonful at a time. Simmer for 4–5 minutes. Add cream and season with salt and pepper.

MAKES 6–8 SERVINGS

Shrimp and Scallop with Tomato and Romano

The shrimp and the scallop, fresh from the sea, come together here to sing a duet in perfect harmony and counterpoint.

¼ cup	clarified butter	50 mL
2	garlic cloves, minced	2
½ cup	chopped onion	125 mL
½ cup	chopped fennel	125 mL
½ cup	diced green pepper	125 mL
1 lb	shrimp, peeled and deveined	500 g
2 Tbsp	chopped fresh oregano	30 mL
6 cups	fresh tomato sauce	1.5 L
1 lb	bay scallops	500 g
3 cups	chicken stock	750 mL
½ cup	grated Romano cheese	125 mL
	salt and crushed chilies to taste	

In a medium-sized soup pot melt butter over medium-high heat. Add garlic, onion, fennel and green pepper and sauté for 2–3 minutes, stirring frequently. Stir in the shrimps and oregano and sauté for 3 minutes. Add tomato sauce and stock, bring to the boil, reduce heat to simmer, add scallops and simmer soup 8 minutes or *just* until scallops are cooked. Stir in Romano cheese. Season with salt if necessary and chilies.

MAKES 8–10 SERVINGS

Fresh Mussels with Green Peppercorns and Cream

The lowly mussel is raised to new heights of splendor in this creamy soup. Its mother would be proud. So will you.

¼ cup	clarified butter	50 mL
½ cup	finely diced red pepper	125 mL
½ cup	chopped onion	125 mL
1	garlic clove, minced	1
1 cup	sliced mushrooms	250 mL
1 Tbsp	green peppercorns in brine	30 mL
1 Tbsp	chopped fresh basil	15 mL
½ cup	dry white wine	125 mL
6 cups	chicken or fish stock	1.5 L
1 lb	fresh live cultured mussels	500 g
3 Tbsp	beurre manié	45 mL
¼ cup	heavy cream (35%)	50 mL
1 Tbsp	Dijon mustard	15 mL

Sauté red pepper, onion, garlic and mushrooms in butter, for 3–4 minutes over medium-high heat. Add peppercorns in brine, basil and wine. Bring to a boil, add the stock and return to a boil. Add the mussels, cover the pot, and cook for 2–3 minutes or until mussels just open. Remove mussels, and bring soup back to a boil.

Meanwhile, in a medium bowl, whisk beurre manié until smooth. Slowly whisk in a cupful of soup then whisk the mixture 1 spoonful at a time back into the soup. Whisk in cream and mustard. Return mussels to pot and serve.

MAKES 4–6 SERVINGS

Clams J. Neale

Of all the soups in Chef Brad's repertoire, this is the publisher's choice as best of the best.

3 Tbsp	clarified butter	40 mL
2 cups	sliced green onion	500 mL
1 cup	sliced onion	250 mL
1 cup	julienned red pepper	250 mL
3 cups	sliced fresh mushrooms	750 mL
3	garlic cloves, minced	3
¼ cup	cognac	50 mL
¼ cup	dry white wine	50 mL
¼ cup	dry sherry	50 mL
1 can	(20 oz/600 g) mandarin oranges with syrup	1 can
1 cup	fresh tomato sauce	250 mL
¼ cup	chopped fresh basil	50 mL
4	saffron strands	4
6 cups	chicken stock	1.5 L
1 cup	chopped sun-dried tomatoes	250 mL
4½ lbs	fresh live clams	2.25 kg

Heat butter in a medium soup pot, add onions, pepper, mushrooms and garlic and sauté for 3–4 minutes. Add cognac, wine and sherry. Bring to a boil and reduce mixture by half. Add oranges and syrup, tomato sauce, basil, saffron, stock and sun-dried tomatoes. Bring to the boil and add clams. Cover and bring back to the boil and cook just until clams open, about 4–6 minutes.

MAKES 8–10 SERVINGS

Snow Crab Rarebit
with Stilton

As delicate as a ballerina in mid-arabesque,
yet as full-bodied as a Rubens model.
Your artistry will win an admiring ovation.

⅓ cup	clarified butter	75 mL
1	garlic clove, minced	1
½ cup	finely diced onion	125 mL
½ cup	finely diced red pimento or red pepper	125 mL
½ cup	diced green pepper	125 mL
½ lb	snow crab meat	250 g
1 tsp	chopped fresh tarragon	5 mL
¼ cup	flat beer*	50 mL
6 cups	chicken or fish stock	1.5 L
5 Tbsp	beurre manié	75 mL
4 oz	Stilton cheese, crumbled	125 g
½ cup	heavy cream (35%)	125 mL
	salt, white pepper and freshly grated nutmeg to taste	

* You can take fresh beer and whisk it to remove the fizz.

Heat butter in a large heavy soup pot. Add garlic, onion, pimento, green pepper and sauté for 3–4 minutes over medium heat or until slightly softened. Break crab meat apart and add to soup pot. Stir in tarragon, beer and stock and bring to boil.

In a medium-sized bowl, whisk beurre manié until smooth. Slowly whisk in a cupful of the soup mixture until beurre manié resembles a smooth paste. Add to the soup 1 spoonful at a time whisking constantly. Simmer gently to thicken slightly. Add Stilton, whisking until completely melted. Stir in cream and season with salt, pepper and nutmeg. Serve.

MAKES 4–6 SERVINGS

Shrimp Bisque

Forget about oysters and any other
aphrodisiacs you may have heard about.
This is the ultimate soup for lovers.
Rich and creamy and just a bit naughty.

2 Tbsp	clarified butter	30 mL
¼ cup	diced carrot	50 mL
¼ cup	chopped onion	50 mL
1 Tbsp	chopped fresh parsley	15 mL
1 tsp	chopped fresh tarragon	5 mL
1	bay leaf	1
1 lb	prawns, peeled and deveined	500 g
1 Tbsp	Armagnac	15 mL
1 cup	dry white wine	250 mL
½ cup	long grain rice	125 mL
3 cups	chicken stock	750 mL
⅓ cup	heavy cream (35%)	75 mL
	salt and white pepper to taste	

In a heavy soup pot melt butter over medium-high heat. Add carrot, onion, parsley, tarragon and bay leaf and sauté until golden brown, about 4 minutes. Add prawns and cook for a couple of minutes. Sprinkle with Armagnac, stir in wine and ½ cup (125 mL) stock. Simmer for 3 minutes or until reduced slightly. Meanwhile in another pot cook the rice in the remaining stock—bringing it to a boil then reducing the heat and simmering it for 15–20 minutes.

Stir the cooked rice into the soup, whisk in cream and season if necessary.

MAKES 2–4 SERVINGS

Crab with Cream and Garlic

An Arctic adventure in a bowl,
irresistibly flavorful and nourishing, belying
the simplicity of its preparation.

¼ cup	clarified butter	50 mL
½ cup	chopped onion	125 mL
3	garlic cloves, minced	3
½ lb	snow crab meat	250 g
5 cups	chicken or fish stock	1.25 L
1 tsp	chopped fresh thyme	5 mL
¼ cup	beurre manié	50 mL
⅓ cup	heavy cream (35%)	75 mL
	salt and pepper to taste	

In a large heavy soup pot add butter and melt over medium-high heat. Add onion and garlic and sauté for 3–4 minutes. Add crab, stock and thyme and bring to the boil.

In a medium-sized bowl, whisk beurre manié until smooth. Slowly whisk in a cupful of the soup mixture until beurre manié resembles a smooth paste. Add to the soup 1 spoonful at a time, whisking constantly. Simmer until thickened slightly. Stir in cream and season with salt and pepper.

MAKES 3–4 SERVINGS

POULTRY AND
GAME SOUPS

Cream of Chicken with Mandarin Orange and Sherry

Just a hint of the Orient and a splash of Mediterranean sunshine to tickle your taste buds and please your palate.

¼ cup	clarified butter	50 mL
2	garlic cloves, minced	2
½ cup	diced onion	125 mL
¼ cup	diced red pepper	50 mL
20 oz	mandarin oranges	600 g
½ cup	fresh orange juice	125 mL
4 cups	chicken stock	1 L
pinch	nutmeg	pinch
pinch	cinnamon	pinch
pinch	ground allspice	pinch
⅓ cup	dry sherry	75 mL
3 Tbsp	beurre manié	45 mL
¼ cup	heavy cream (35%)	50 mL
	salt and pepper to taste	

In a medium soup pot heat butter over medium heat. Add garlic, onion, red pepper and sauté for 3–4 minutes. Add oranges, orange juice and stock and bring to a boil, then reduce heat and simmer for 4–5 minutes. Stir in nutmeg, cinnamon, allspice and sherry.

Meanwhile in a small bowl whisk beurre manié until smooth. Slowly whisk in a cupful of soup. Whisk mixture back into soup 1 spoonful at a time and simmer for 3–4 minutes or until thickened slightly. Whisk in cream and season with salt and pepper

MAKES 4–6 SERVINGS

Smoked Chicken Florentine

Popeye would approve. Not only is his favorite strength-giving vegetable liberally employed here but no olive oil is required.

¼ cup	clarified butter	50 mL
1½ lbs	smoked chicken, cut into ¼-inch cubes	750 g
½ cup	diced onion	125 mL
1	garlic clove, minced	1
¼ cup	white wine	50 mL
8 cups	chicken stock	2 L
2 lbs	spinach, cleaned and chopped	1 kg
½ cup	chopped fresh basil	125 mL
2	eggs, beaten lightly	2
½ cup	grated Parmesan cheese	125 mL
	white pepper to taste	

Heat butter in a medium soup pot over medium-high heat. Add chicken, onion, garlic and sauté for 2–3 minutes or until the onion wilts slightly. Add wine and stock, bring to a boil then reduce heat and simmer for 3 minutes. Add spinach and basil and simmer for 4–5 minutes, stirring occasionally. Whisk in beaten eggs then Parmesan cheese. Season with pepper.

MAKES 8 SERVINGS

Smoked Chicken with Raspberries and Sherry

*The quintessential soup for all seasons —
wonderfully warming on a cold winter's day,
refreshingly cool in summer.*

¼ cup	clarified butter	50 mL
¼ cup	diced onion	50 mL
1 lb	diced smoked chicken	500 g
2 cups	fresh raspberries	500 mL
¼ cup	sherry	50 mL
4 cups	chicken stock	1 L
1 tsp	chopped rosemary	5 mL
¼ cup	sour cream (optional)	50 mL
	salt and white pepper to taste	

Heat butter in a medium-sized soup pot over medium-high heat. Add onion, chicken and raspberries, and sauté for 2 minutes, stirring constantly. Deglaze the pan with sherry and add the stock and rosemary. Bring to a boil, then reduce the heat to simmer for 5 minutes. Season with salt and white pepper.

Serve with a dollop of sour cream.

MAKES 4–6 SERVINGS

Spicy Tandoori Chicken

This spicy concoction will lead your taste buds in a tango. Chicken soup has rarely been so sexy and sensuous.

¼ cup	clarified butter	50 mL
2 cups	boneless chicken, cut into 1-inch cubes	500 mL
½ cup	coarsely chopped celery	125 mL
½ cup	coarsely chopped red pepper	125 mL
½ cup	coarsely chopped green pepper	125 mL
½ cup	chopped onion	125 mL
1	garlic clove, minced	1
2 tsp	tomato paste	10 mL
¼ cup	Basmati rice	50 mL
2 tsp	tandoori barbecue powder	10 mL
4 cups	chicken stock	750 mL
	salt and pepper to taste	

In a small soup pot melt the butter over medium heat. Add the chicken, celery, peppers, onion and garlic and sauté for 4–5 minutes. Add the tomato paste and rice and sauté for 2 minutes more, stirring constantly. Stir in the tandoori barbecue powder and chicken stock. Bring to a boil, then reduce the heat and simmer for 18–20 minutes. Season with salt and pepper.

MAKES 4 SERVINGS

Pheasant with Fresh Peaches and Sherry

The favorite game bird of British royalty and nobility in a creation that's truly fit for a king or queen. Bracing, what?

For Stock

1	pheasant (approx 1½ lbs/750 g)	1
¼ cup	port wine	50 mL
1	carrot, peeled and finely diced	1
1	onion, finely diced	1
1	leek, finely diced	1

For Soup

¼ cup	clarified butter	50 mL
¼ cup	diced onion	50 mL
¼ cup	finely diced red pepper	50 mL
1	garlic clove, minced	1
1 Tbsp	tomato paste	15 mL
3	peaches, peeled, pitted and cut into eighths	3
2 Tbsp	marmalade	30 mL
½ tsp	thyme	2 mL
⅓ cup	sherry	75 mL
2 Tbsp	beurre manié	30 mL
¼ cup	heavy cream (35%)	50 mL
	salt and pepper to taste	

Roast pheasant in a preheated 400°F (200°C) oven for 35 minutes. Cool and debone, reserving meat for soup. For stock: deglaze the pan by placing it on top of a burner over medium-high heat. Add the port and scrape up the bits. Add bones and deglazed liquid to a medium-sized soup pot. Add carrot, onion, leek and 8 cups (2 L) water. Bring to a boil, reduce the heat and simmer for 1½ hours. Strain.

For soup, heat the butter in a small soup pot. Add onion, red pepper and garlic and sauté for 2 minutes. Add reserved pheasant meat, tomato paste, peaches, marmalade, thyme, sherry and stock. Bring to a boil, reduce heat and simmer for 8–10 minutes.

In a small bowl whisk beurre manié until smooth. Slowly whisk in a cupful of soup and whisk back into soup 1 spoonful at a time. Simmer for 5 minutes or until thickened slightly. Whisk in cream and season with salt and pepper.

MAKES 4–6 SERVINGS

Consommé
et Chasseur

*An appetizing reminder of the vast Canadian
wilderness, matchless in the beauty and serenity of its
deep, dark lakes and majestic mountains and forests.*

1 lb	mixed game flesh, finely ground	500 g
1	leek, coarsely chopped	1
1 tsp	finely chopped rosemary	5 mL
1 tsp	finely chopped sage	5 mL
6	juniper berries, whole	6
2	egg whites	2
6 cups	game stock	1.5 L
12	bolet mushrooms, sliced	12
⅓ cup	port	75 mL

In a stock pot mix together meat, leek, rosemary, sage,
juniper berries and egg whites. Add stock and bring
mixture just to a boil, then reduce heat and simmer gently
for 2 hours. *Do not stir* so as not to disturb the cap of impu-
rities. Gently break open an area of the cap and ladle out
the clean stock. Discard the rest.

Meanwhile, in a small saucepan, pour the port over the
sliced mushrooms. Over medium heat, bring just to a boil,
then reduce the heat and poach for 1–2 minutes. Add to
the consommé.

MAKES 4 SERVINGS

HEARTY MEAT
SOUPS

French Lamb au Gratin

C'est si bon! This will win the same rave reviews on your dining room table that it would get from the most knowledgeable of food critics in Normandy.

¼ cup	clarified butter	50 mL
40	pearl onions, peeled	40
2 lbs	boneless leg of lamb, roasted and cut in ½-inch cubes	1 kg
¼ cup	dry red wine	50 mL
1 tsp	chopped fresh thyme	5 mL
1 tsp	chopped fresh rosemary	5 mL
1	garlic clove, minced	1
2 Tbsp	tomato paste	30 mL
5 cups	lamb stock	1.25 L
8	slices french stick	8
1 cup	grated Swiss cheese	250 mL
¼ cup	grated Parmesan	50 mL
¼ cup	port wine	50 mL

Heat the butter in a medium soup pot, add onions and brown lightly, stirring occasionally. Add lamb and brown well. Stir in wine, thyme, rosemary, garlic and tomato paste. Add stock and simmer 8–10 minutes.

Meanwhile make croutons by toasting bread circles until browned on both sides.

Spoon soup into eight oven-proof crocks. Mix cheese together. Place a crouton on top of each soup crock, top with cheese and broil until browned and bubbly. Splash with port and serve.

MAKES 8 SERVINGS

Con Carne Soup

*Be forewarned: Chef Brad's chili has caused water
shortages in the area of the St. Lawrence Market.
So if hot and spicy is what you like, then olé!*

¼ cup	clarified butter	50 mL
2 lbs	medium ground beef	1 kg
2	garlic cloves, minced	2
1½ cups	chopped green pepper	375 mL
1 cup	chopped onion	250 mL
1 cup	chopped leek	250 mL
4 cups	tomato sauce	1 L
3 cups	tomato juice	750 mL
¼ cup	ketchup	50 mL
½ tsp	chopped fresh thyme	2 mL
½ tsp	chopped fresh oregano	2 mL
½ tsp	chopped fresh basil	2 mL
6–8	chilies, whole	6–8
1 Tbsp	Mexican chili powder	15 mL
1 Tbsp	Worcestershire sauce	15 mL
19 oz	canned red kidney beans	585 g
	freshly ground black pepper to taste	

Heat butter in large soup pot, add beef and brown, about
5–6 minutes. Add garlic, pepper, onion and leek and sauté

for 2–3 minutes. Add tomato sauce, tomato juice, ketchup and herbs, chilies, chili powder and Worcestershire sauce, bring to a boil, then reduce heat and simmer for 20 minutes, stirring occasionally. Add beans and season with pepper.

MAKES 8 SERVINGS

Ground Pork Szechuan

What to serve at your pre-theatre dinner prior to seeing Miss Saigon or Madame Butterfly? You couldn't make a more appropriate — or delectable — choice.

¼ cup	peanut or soy bean oil	50 mL
1 lb	ground pork	500 g
½ cup	julienned red peppers	125 mL
½ cup	coarsely chopped celery, cut on the diagonal	125 mL
3	garlic cloves, minced	3
½ cup	sliced onion	125 mL
¼ cup	sliced leek	50 mL
1 tsp	hoisin sauce	5 mL
pinch	five spice powder	pinch
1 Tbsp	ketchup	15 mL
1 Tbsp	soy sauce	15 mL
3 Tbsp	Vietnamese chili sauce	45 mL
3 cups	chicken stock	750 mL
1 Tbsp	cornstarch, mixed with 2–3 Tbsp (30–45 mL) cold water	15 mL

Heat oil in a large wok over high heat. Add the pork and brown, stirring constantly for 6–8 minutes. Add red pepper, celery, garlic, onion and leek and sauté for 2–3 minutes, stirring constantly. Stir in hoisin, five spice powder, ketchup, soy, and chili sauce and then add stock. Bring to a boil and whisk in cornstarch mixture. Reduce heat and simmer 2 minutes or until thickened slightly. Serve.

MAKES 4–6 SERVINGS.

Peppersteak Soup

A manly soup. But women love it, too. It's as robust as a lineman on a Grey Cup-winning team yet as artful as an Olympic gymnast.

¼ cup	clarified butter	50 mL
2 lbs	top sirloin steak, cut in ½-inch cubes	1 kg
2 Tbsp	diced dry porcini mushrooms	30 mL
10	mushrooms, sliced	10
20	red peppercorns	20
1 tsp	cracked black peppercorns	5 mL
1 Tbsp	green peppercorns in brine	15 mL
¼ cup	diced green pepper	50 mL
¼ cup	diced red pepper	50 mL
½ cup	diced onion	125 mL
2	garlic cloves, minced	2
1 Tbsp	fresh thyme	15 mL
½ cup	dry red wine	125 mL
2 Tbsp	chili sauce	30 mL
7 cups	beef stock	1.75 L
2 Tbsp	dark roux	30 mL
8 tsp	sour cream	40 mL
	salt and pepper to taste	

In a medium-sized soup pot heat butter over medium-high heat, then add steak and brown. Add mushrooms, peppercorns, peppers, onion, garlic and thyme and continue cooking for about 6 minutes stirring frequently. Deglaze the pan with red wine, mustard, chili sauce and stock. Bring to a boil, reduce heat and simmer for 5 minutes.

Meanwhile in a small bowl whisk the roux while slowly adding a cupful of soup. Whisk back into soup 1 spoonful at a time. Season with salt and pepper and simmer for 5 minutes or until thickened slightly. Serve with a dollop of sour cream.

MAKES 8 SERVINGS

Hungarian Cabbage with Ground Beef

*Only those who might be able to resist
tapping their toes to the strains of gypsy violins
should resist the opportunity to try this wild
and wonderful taste treat.*

¼ cup	olive oil	50 mL
1 lb	lean ground beef	500 g
3	garlic cloves, minced	3
½ cup	diced onion	125 mL
½ cup	diced green pepper	125 mL
½ cup	diced red pepper	125 mL
½ cup	chopped leek	125 mL
5 cups	shredded cabbage	1.125 L
½ cup	white wine sauerkraut, drained	125 mL
½ cup	long grain white rice	125 mL
2 cups	tomato sauce	500 mL
8 cups	chicken stock	2 L
	salt and pepper to taste	

Heat oil in a medium-sized soup pot. Add ground beef and cook for 5–6 minutes stirring frequently until browned. Add garlic, onion, peppers, leek, cabbage, sauerkraut and rice and continue to sauté for 3–4 minutes. Add tomato sauce and stock, bring to the boil then reduce the heat and simmer for 20 minutes. Serve.

MAKES 8–10 SERVINGS

Spicy Spanish Chorizo Soup

Picture in your mind's eye the spiciest of Pablo Picasso's etchings — The Minotaur's Orgies, for example. Here it is in liquid form.

¼ cup	clarified butter	50 mL
½ cup	sliced onion	125 mL
½ cup	julienned green pepper	125 mL
1	garlic clove, minced	1
½ cup	sliced celery	125 mL
6	dried chili peppers	6
2 cups	sliced dried chorizo sausage	500 mL
6	fennel seeds	6
2 tsp	chopped fresh coriander	10 mL
3 cups	fresh tomato sauce	750 mL
2 cups	chicken stock	500 mL
	salt and pepper to taste	

Heat butter in a medium-sized soup pot. Add onion, pepper, garlic, celery and chili peppers and sauté for 4–5 minutes, stirring occasionally. Add sausage, fennel seeds, coriander, tomato sauce and chicken stock. Bring to the boil, then reduce heat and simmer for 8–10 minutes. Season with salt and pepper.

MAKES 4–6 SERVINGS

West Indian Pepperpot

Picture yourself soaking up the sunshine on a palm-fringed Caribbean beach to the accompaniment of a reggae band. It's hot and spicy, mon.

1½ lbs	short ribs, ¼-inch thick, cut into 2-inch pieces	750 g
½ cup	red wine	125 mL
2	large carrots, peeled and sliced	2
1	large potato, peeled and diced	1
2	scotch bonnet peppers	2
½ cup	diced green pepper	125 mL
½ cup	sliced leek	125 mL
1	garlic clove, minced	1
3	anise stars	3
1	small cinnamon stick	1
1 tsp	finely chopped thyme	15 mL
10 cups	cold water	2.25 L
2 Tbsp	long grain white or brown rice	30 mL
	salt and pepper to taste	

Roast short ribs in a preheated 350°F (180°C) oven for 30 minutes or until browned. Deglaze the roasting pan with red wine. Place short ribs, wine, carrot, potato, peppers, leek, garlic, anise, cinnamon, thyme and water into a large soup pot. Bring to a boil, then reduce the heat and simmer for 40–50 minutes. Add the rice and simmer for another 20 minutes. Season with salt and pepper.

MAKES 8–10 SERVINGS

Flank Steak with Hoisin and Peppers

*As peppy as a Nissan 300 ZX, it will put
your appetite in overdrive. If there were an
Indianapolis 500 for soups, this would be
an odds-on favorite.*

¼ cup	soya bean or peanut oil	50 mL
1½ lbs	flank steak, cut into strips	750 g
½ cup	julienned leek	125 mL
½ cup	julienned red pepper	125 mL
½ cup	julienned green pepper	125 mL
2 Tbsp	julienned jalapeno peppers	30 mL
1	garlic clove, minced	1
1 tsp	ginger, finely chopped	5 mL
	juice of ½ lemon	
pinch	Chinese five spice powder	pinch
1 Tbsp	hoisin sauce	15 mL
1 Tbsp	Vietnamese chili sauce	15 mL
3 cups	beef stock	750 mL
2 Tbsp	beurre manié	30 mL
	salt and pepper to taste	

Heat oil in a medium soup pot over medium-high heat.
Stir-fry steak, stirring constantly for 2–3 minutes. Add
leek, peppers, garlic and ginger. Continue to stir-fry for
2–3 minutes. Add lemon juice, Chinese five spice, hoisin
and Vietnamese chili sauce and stock. Bring to the boil.

Meanwhile in a small bowl whisk beurre manié until smooth. Slowly whisk in a cupful of soup until smooth. Whisk back into soup 1 spoonful at a time. Cook for 2–3 minutes or until thickened slightly. Season with salt and pepper.

MAKES 4 SERVINGS

English Stew
from Ground Beef

*The tastiest of English pub fare, so easily
prepared and so heartily enjoyed. Serve during
the Super Bowl or Stanley Cup playoffs.
A guaranteed winner.*

½ cup	clarified butter	125 mL
1½ lbs	lean ground beef	750 g
½ cup	tomato concassée	125 mL
½ cup	diced green pepper	125 mL
½ cup	diced carrot	125 mL
½ cup	diced onion	125 mL
½ cup	diced leek	125 mL
1	garlic clove, minced	1
½ tsp	chopped thyme	2 mL
4 cups	beef stock	1 L
1 Tbsp	Dijon mustard	15 mL
⅓ cup	sour cream	75 mL
	salt and pepper to taste	

Melt butter in a medium soup pot on medium temperature. Add beef and cook, stirring occasionally until browned, about 8–10 minutes. Add tomato concassée, green pepper, carrot, onion, leek and garlic and sauté for 4–5 minutes. Add thyme and stock, bring to boil, then reduce the heat and simmer for 8–10 minutes. Whisk in mustard and season with salt and pepper. To serve, ladle into soup bowls and spoon on a dollop of sour cream.

MAKES 3–4 SERVINGS

Cream of Sauerkraut with Double Smoked Pork

*This soup is never served before
a long journey.*

¼ cup	clarified butter	50 mL
½ cup	diced carrots	125 mL
½ cup	diced green pepper	125 mL
½ cup	diced leek	125 mL
1 cup	double smoked bacon, cut in ¼-inch pieces	250 mL
½ cup	sliced mushrooms	125 mL
1	garlic clove, minced	1
1 cup	white wine sauerkraut	250 mL
8	juniper berries	8
½ tsp	chopped fresh rosemary	2 mL
4 cups	chicken stock	1 L
2 Tbsp	beurre manié	30 mL
¼ cup	heavy cream (35%)	50 mL
	salt and pepper to taste	

Heat butter in a soup pot. Add the carrot, pepper, leek and bacon and sauté for 2–3 minutes. Add the mushrooms, garlic, sauerkraut, juniper berries and rosemary and sauté for 2–3 minutes. Stir in the stock, then bring to a boil and reduce the heat to simmer.

Meanwhile in a small bowl whisk beurre manié until smooth. Slowly whisk in a cupful of soup until a smooth paste is formed. Whisk 1 spoonful of the mixture at a time into the soup and cook until thickened slightly. Stir in cream and season with salt and pepper.

MAKES 4 SERVINGS

Lamb Porcini

Think spring. Think of lilacs and forsythia in bloom and of clear blue skies dotted with fluffy white clouds. Now drink deeply of these delights.

1 oz	dried porcini mushrooms	30 g
⅓ cup	red wine	75 mL
¼ cup	clarified butter	50 mL
1½ lbs	lamb, cut into ½-inch cubes	750 g
1	garlic clove, minced	1
½ cup	diced onion	125 mL
½ cup	diced leek	125 mL
½ cup	diced green pepper	125 mL
1 tsp	chopped thyme	5 mL
3	bay leaves	3
6 cups	lamb or beef stock	1.5 L
¼ cup	pearl barley	50 mL
1 cup	tomato sauce	250 mL
½ cup	chopped sun-dried tomatoes	125 mL
	salt and pepper to taste	

Cover mushrooms with wine and let soak for 1 hour.

Heat butter in a medium-sized soup pot. Add the lamb and brown, stirring occasionally. Add the garlic, onion, leek, green pepper, thyme and bay leaves and sauté for 2–3 minutes, stirring occasionally. Add mushrooms, wine and stock and bring to a boil. Reduce heat to simmer and stir in the barley, tomato sauce, and sun-dried tomatoes. Simmer for 20–30 minutes. Season with salt and pepper.

MAKES 6–8 SERVINGS

Old Fashioned Short Rib Stew

"Everything old is new again," so it's said.
And for a cool autumn or cold winter's night, this
meal-in-a-bowl will please both young and old.

2½ lbs	short ribs, cut into ½-inch thick pieces	1.25 kg
2 Tbsp	red wine	30 mL
3	tomatoes, peeled, seeded and chopped	3
1	medium potato, coarsely chopped	1
1 cup	coarsely chopped parsnip	250 mL
½ cup	sliced carrot	125 mL
½ cup	coarsely chopped zucchini	125 mL
½ cup	coarsely chopped squash	125 mL
3	garlic cloves, minced	3
2 Tbsp	barley	30 mL
½ tsp	chopped fresh thyme	2 mL
½ tsp	chopped fresh tarragon	2 mL
8 cups	cold water	2 L
	salt and pepper to taste	

Bake the short ribs for 45–60 minutes in a preheated 400°F (200°C) oven. Once fully browned, place the ribs in a large stewing pot. Deglaze the roasting pan with red wine, then add the mixture to the stewing pot with the remaining ingredients. Bring to a boil, then reduce the heat and simmer for 1 hour. Season with salt and pepper.

MAKES 8–10 SERVINGS

Loin of Pork with Fresh Raspberries

Like Bogie and Bacall, Charles and Di, Brian and Mila, pork and fresh-picked raspberries make an unlikely but winning combo.

⅓ cup	clarified butter	75 mL
1½ lbs	pork loin, cut into ¼-inch cubes	750 g
½ cup	diced green pepper	125 mL
½ cup	diced onion	125 mL
1	garlic clove, minced	1
2 cups	fresh raspberries	500 mL
1 tsp	chopped fresh dill	5 mL
¼ cup	dry sherry	50 mL
4 cups	chicken stock	1 L
	salt and white pepper to taste	

Heat butter in a medium-sized soup pot over medium heat. Add the pork and cook for 4–5 minutes. Pour off excess fat, then add green pepper, onion, garlic, raspberries and dill. Sauté for 2–3 minutes. Deglaze the pot with sherry. Add the stock and bring to a boil. Reduce the heat and simmer for 8–10 minutes. Season with salt and pepper.

MAKES 4 SERVINGS

CHILLED
SOUPS

Guacamole Soup with Fresh Oysters and Shrimp

A trio of delights, one fresh off the tree, two fresh from the sea, brought together as the perfect combination to lead into a light summertime meal.

3	ripe avocados, peeled and pit removed	3
	juice of 2 lemons	
1	garlic clove, minced	1
1 tsp	finely chopped dill	5 mL
1 Tbsp	finely diced pimento stuffed olives	15 mL
2 cups	10% cream	500 mL
2 dashes	Worcestershire sauce	2 dashes
4 dashes	Tabasco sauce	4 dashes
	salt and pepper to taste	
24	oysters, shucked, with their juice	24
6	cooked shrimp, finely diced	6

Place the avocado flesh in the bowl of a food processor fitted with a steel blade. Add lemon juice and garlic and process for 2–3 minutes or until smooth. Remove avocado mixture to a large bowl. Whisk in dill, olives, cream, Worcestershire sauce, Tabasco, salt and pepper. Stir in oysters and their juice. Ladle into soup bowls and garnish with shrimp.

MAKES 4–5 SERVINGS

Chilled Pureé of Apple with Pineapple, Mint and Calvados

A perfectly refreshing summertime treat, so easy to prepare, so tasty to enjoy. As smooth as a waltz by Strauss.

½	small pineapple, peeled, cored and puréed	½
2	tart apples, peeled, cored and puréed	2
	juice of ½ lemon	
1 cup	sour cream	250 mL
3 Tbsp	Calvados	45 mL
2 cups	milk	500 mL
1 Tbsp	chopped fresh mint	15 mL

Combine all ingredients in a large bowl and whisk together. Refrigerate for 12 hours so that the flavors blend. Whisk well again and serve.

MAKES 4–6 SERVINGS

Chilled Strawberry Soup with Baby Shrimp and Lox

*So rich and so refreshing, you might be tempted
to serve it for dessert rather than as a starter.
Very cool. Very 1990s.*

2 cups	fresh strawberries, washed and hulled	500 mL
2 cups	sour cream	500 mL
1½ oz	smoked salmon, julienned	45 g
¾ lb	baby or cocktail shrimp	375 g
	juice of 1 lemon	
2 Tbsp	fresh chopped mint	30 mL
4 cups	10% cream	1 L
1 Tbsp	white sugar	15 mL
¼ cup	dry sherry	50 mL

Place strawberries in the bowl of food processor or blender.
Process until very smooth. Pour into a large bowl. Whisk in
remaining ingredients and chill 12 hours before serving.

MAKES 8–10 SERVINGS

Chilled Orange and Kiwi with Crushed Pecans and Grand Marnier

Picture a golf course on a summer's day with the dew glistening on the fresh-mown fairways and birds singing in the trees. Now taste it.

2 cups	freshly squeezed orange juice	500 mL
1 cup	sour cream	250 mL
3	ripe kiwi, peeled and puréed	3
½ cup	pecan pieces	125 mL
¼ cup	Grand Marnier	50 mL
1 Tbsp	fresh dill, finely chopped	15 mL
2 cups	10% cream	500 mL
pinch	nutmeg	pinch
pinch	cinnamon	pinch

Combine all ingredients in a bowl. Whisk well. Chill 12 hours then whisk well again. Add nutmeg and cinnamon and serve.

MAKES 4–6 SERVINGS

Chilled Pineapple and Strawberry with Kirsch

Let the kids eat popsicles. But for the more sophisticated palate this is the ultimate in refreshment for the "lazy, hazy, crazy days of summer."

4 cups	strawberries, washed and hulled	1 L
1	pineapple, peeled and cut in chunks	1
1 cup	sour cream	250 mL
3 cups	10% cream	750 mL
2 tsp	white sugar	10 mL
3 Tbsp	chopped fresh dill	45 mL
⅓ cup	Kirsch	75 mL

Place the strawberries and pineapple in the bowl of a food processor. Whir 3 minutes or until smooth.

Place sour cream in a large bowl. Slowly whisk in the fruit purée then the cream. Season with sugar, dill and Kirsch. Chill and serve.

MAKES 8–10 SERVINGS

Index

INDEX

with two mushrooms in red
wine, 20
with yellow ceps and red wine, 25
Seafood soups, 15-36
B.C. salmon with saffron and
lemon juice, 22
clams J. Neale, 30
crab à la king, 18
crab with cream and garlic, 36
cream of smoked salmon with
fresh dill and cognac, 23
fresh mussels with green peppercorns and cream, 28
fresh tuna with whole capers and
sherry, 16
marlin with green olives and
cream, 26
scallops with two mushrooms in
red wine, 20
scallops with yellow ceps and
red wine, 25
shrimp and scallops with tomato
and Romano, 27
shrimp bisque, 34
snow crab rarebit with
Stilton, 32
tandoori lobster with red lentils, 24
Short ribs. See beef.
Shrimp bisque, 34
Shrimps
with scallops, tomato and
Romano, 27
with strawberries and lox, 74
Sirloin steak. See beef.
Smoked chicken
florentine, 40
with raspberries and sherry, 41
Smoked pork. See pork.
Smoked salmon. See salmon.
Snow crab rarebit with Stilton, 32
Spanish onion and bean soup, 8
Spicy Spanish chorizo soup, 57
Spicy tandoori chicken, 42
Spinach with smoked chicken, 40
Stilton cheese with snow crab, 32
Stock, xii-xiii
beef, xv
chicken, xvi
fish, xiv

game, xiv
Strawberries
with lentils and smoked pork, 4
with pineapple and Kirsch, 76
with shrimp and lox, 74
Sun-dried tomatoes. See tomatoes,
sun-dried.

T
Tandoori lobster with red lentils, 24
Tomatoes
concassée with oyster
mushrooms, 10
with Romano, shrimp and
scallops, 27
sun-dried
with clams, 30
with lamb porcini, 66
Tuna, fresh, with capers and sherry,
16

V
Vegetable soups, 2-14
Belgian endive with lemon, lime
and cream, 5
braised garlic bordelaise, 14
corn with fresh basil and
lemon, 6
cream of Brussels sprouts and
Gorgonzola, 11
French onion with whole spring
onions, 2
Greek eggplant soup, 7
lentils with smoked pork and
strawberries, 4
olde fashioned corn chowder, 12
oyster mushrooms with tomato, 10
Spanish onion and bean soup, 8
whole mushrooms in broth, 9
Vermicelli with Brussels sprouts and
Gorgonzola, 11

W
West Indian pepperpot, 58
Whole mushrooms in broth, 9

Y
Yellow cep mushrooms with scallops
and red wine, 25